# Praise for *Sum of Worlds*

Naima Rashid's *Sum of Worlds* takes readers on a journey through the fabric of human experience, woven as it is with delicate threads of memory, emotion, and introspection. Rashid's poems paint vivid portraits of characters grappling with the complexities of life, love, and loss. Rather than simply adding up or subtracting her literary realms, the poet instead enters the intimate spaces of individuals whose lives intersect with the fabric of history, tradition, and personal struggle. Through lyrical vignettes, she explores themes of identity, resilience, and the enduring power of human connection. This is recommended reading for poetry lovers.

—Claire Chambers, Professor of Global Literature, University of York

While there is so much to admire in this gorgeous collection of poems, I was most struck by the theme of parenthood that makes its way into many of them—the terrifying joy and heartbreak of it, the unbearability of the role that so many of us bear. From aphoristic little gems to meandering poems that reward patience with insight and wisdom, this collection has it all. It was a thrill to read it."

—Dur e Aziz Amna, author of *American Fever*

I love Naima Rashid's emotive poetry. Truth is at the very heart of her work and the unusual images she conjures stay with the reader. Her poems reflect multiplicity and plurality both thematically and linguistically because her great subject is humanity itself, with all its complexities and nuances. Her unique idiom is enriched by her multi-lingual aesthetic, which permeates her work.

—Faiqa Mansab, author of *This House of Clay and Water*

Rashid writes with a direct voice, displaying a rare attachment to ordinary beauties -- lullaby, yarn, silence, souvenirs, grass, sunlight, and the musings on love and loss -- and indeed brings to life (or, to her/our) bones 'a knowledge of rain'. There is defiance as well as longing in these poems that are woven together with the poet's cultural sensibilities.

—Nabina Das, author of *Anima and the Narrative Limits*

Rashid's poems are devastating, immediate, angry, and pulsating with an energy that took my breath away.

—Shazaf Fatima, author of *A Woman on a Suitcase*

*Sum of Worlds* by Naima Rashid is a sharp and intricate mosaic of lived experience, shimmering with beauty, pain, and resilience. Both the universal and personal come to life in poems that explore and honor family, the self, faith, culture, and society. Through imagery and language that shock the reader into awareness, Rashid reminds us that the journey towards acceptance and peace is a difficult yet rewarding one.

—Shikha Malaviya, author of *Anandibai Joshee:*
*A Life in Poems*

Forget the milk, get the daffodils and wander into the vivid and wild imaginarium that is the sum of Naima Rashid's worlds, where you will find a female ancestor who is a" broker of brocades" and a migraine  that is a "galloping elephant". Here, to be well behaved is to be a" gladiator trapped in a tiffin", a

fallen tooth is "a neat square of absence" on a "window face" of
the poet's son. Shot through this weave like a thread of blood
is the pain of migration, exile and being female in a deeply
patriarchal society. Parts of *Sum of Worlds* will shock you but
it is a deeply necessary shock.
—Sophia Naz, author of Bark Archipelago

*Sum of Worlds* brings together experiences of a life parceled
out in the many worlds that boundaries and migrations, cus-
tom and convention, choice and accident stage for us. These
are unadorned poems of everyday experiences and many
voices but smoldering and insurgent in their defiance of can't
and thoughtless supposition. They challenge the curbs and
constraints of tradition and practice, and the suspicions and
divisions the powerplay of family dynamics, colonization,
and politics breeds. Naima Rashid is fearless in exposing the
manipulative and suffocating regimens that mark our pri-
vate and public patterns of living and has an enviable gift of
transforming the commonplace and familiar into a metaphor-
ical reflection of profound truths. Her art lies in making the
ordinary luminous and vibrant with meaning, and she does
this in language that is deceptively simple on its surface. An
exhilarating collection shot through with wisdom and insight.
—Waqas Khwaja, Poet, Professor of English,<br>Agnes Scott College

# Sum of Worlds

# Sum of Worlds

## *Poems*

by

## Naima Rashid

YODA PRESS
C 28 Mayfair Gardens
New Delhi 110 016
www.yodapress.co.in



ISBN 978-93-82579-97-7

Editors in charge: Arpita Das, Soumya Jayanti and Srishti Khare
Typeset in Adobe Garamond Pro, 11/14.4
By mSourcing e-Solutions
Published by Arpita Das and Ishita Gupta for YODA PRESS

*For Bee,*
*moving through his own worlds*

# Contents

# Acknowledgments

I'd like to thank these print and online journals and physical spaces for being the first homes of many of these poems.

Several of these poems appeared for the first time in these excellent journals:

*RIC Journal, The Punch, The Aleph Review, Lucy Writers' Platform, Wild Court, Last Leaves Mag, Poetry at Sangam, Blackbough Poems, Sky Island Journal, One Hand Clapping, Poetry at Sangam, Volume Poetry and Rise Up Review.*

Some poems from the collection were also performed at Heartspoken Word open mic events at Bow Arts, London, curated by Maliha Haider.

On page 61, in the poem 'Continents Breaking', the line '*Le temps est assassin/Et emporte avec lui le rire des enfants/Et les mistrals gagnants*' is taken from the song 'Mistral gagnant' by Renaud Séchan, from the album of the same name released by Virgin Records in 1985.

# Weave

Like a broker of brocades,
a sea of cloth around her,
it was always like this that I found her,
rosary still in hand,
prayer still on lips.
She was a devotee simply continuing
an act of worship.
I came to her temple
like a heathen at a wrong address,
with a kind of dread
and a kind of awe.

She would ease into it gently,
begin unfurling the mounds of memories.
The tea towels were her wedding gift from an uncle
who wore the tallest turban in the village,
who walked on foot in his polished black shoes
all the miles to the village
where he had fallen in love with a married woman,
whom he ultimately made his bride.

You could find them no more,
these khais from Faisalabad,
her nieces had hand-woven them on a spindle;
they had a rare weave.
The nieces don't talk to her anymore because of a family feud;
these are all she has of them.

I couldn't trawl that mine of memories
across the mountains I have to trek,
and the oceans I have to sail.
The sum of my life
fits snugly in a North Face bag.

These pieces were not other from her;
her soul was grafted on to them;
the way she would caress the cotton,
slide her hands over the silk,
touch the tassels of a gifted prayer rug,
she was honoring the souls of the gifters,
catching the breath of the parted ones,
touching up in her mind
the homes of those to come.

And all this while I'm thinking
Isn't she planting a garden of pressed flowers,
plucked from between the pages of time?
Why isn't she more interested in buds?

A macramé that was the only adornment
she could afford in their first house
which they rented at ten rupees a month,

a wedding dress with hair-like golden thread
at the helm – the only object she carried
when they fled Ludhiana for Lahore,
embroidered platitudes she sold
to make ends meet.
The fabric was fraught with her fight,
it held the stories she knew would never
make it into history books.

Her legacy was sprawled around her,
the question trembled in her eyes.
I couldn't bring myself to look up,
lest she read that
I am no worthy care taker
of this sea of yards and yarns.
My style is cross-body;
I live hands-free.

# Migraine

a furrow blazing down the middle of the head
tractors racing down that track
a stampede of elephants running like leopards
devils in togas
beating drums as high as castle walls

# Yards of Plenty

when the shopkeeper removes
one piece from the neatly ordered
wildly blossoming stack
and flicks it open as you sit
it's a yard of stars and dreams that unfurls
dancey shimmery kilometers
a winding milky way
in the bloom of irridescent spring
fest of colours
tango of geometries
all shades confused
all moods cooking up a springy stew
birds and flowers
big and small
tireless trails of tendrils
across salamander miles of dreams
columns of paisleys
like obedient orderlies
there is no dream
that cannot fit in your breadth

no colour too low, too loud for your composition
no bird or blossom
that your bounteous glades can't embrace

I am buying a promise of plenty
a reminder of abundance

I am cutting a robe
out of a field of dreams

# Nani Never Lies

one day, after the weeping stopped
and i had howled my throat dry
i went to nani in her corner room and
asked her straight
'are all souls white in colour?'
she had looked up from her quran
and touched a cloudy wisp of white in her head
'as white as this,' she had said
'even those who are dark of skin on earth?'
'yes, but beti, why do you ask?'

my swollen eyes must have betrayed my grief
to her wisdom vast as the seas
'remember, it doesn't matter what others say or
how they tease you. what matters is here,' she touched
her heart with her trembling hand and tapped it
once
twice
thrice
then placed it on my thundering one 'and there.'

she raised a finger and her head towards the ceiling

but the words did matter
they never stopped stabbing
they never stopped stinging

there were only so many stashes of medicine in the house
i had gone on a rampage of all four floors—
pink, yellow, blue, and white, whole-coloured,
     split-colored—
took a goddamned jug to flush them down
was bloated like a fish when the work was done
my tummy felt
like a birthday balloon
full of stones
that was my ticket and I sat waiting
like a beer-bellied fish
to be borne into the world where
all souls were white
nani had promised
she always kept her word

# Battle for Sky

There's a skyscraper growing in my back yard
like a cranky potted plant.
I'm afraid when it's done,
it will steal
my windowful of sky.

# Garland

She's still young to it—
this body that she wears like a garland.
It hasn't started slashing her skin
through the gaze of others—
still too early for her to tell
the glint of lust apart.

She wears it lightly still,
twirling in its sheerness
like a drape of beauty.
She hasn't started paying the price
for being born into it yet,
bled away what must be bled
to cleanse the curse.

Her body is still body only,
it hasn't crawled into her mind
like cancer.
Her step is still sprightly,
a touch of spring in it,

unbogged by sandbags.
She skips child-like,
has much too spunk to shuffle.

Her waist is twist of ribbon still—
unmarred by battle scars.

She's still young to it—
this body that she wears like a garland.
Matter of time before she learns
it must be borne like a cross.

# Truman Meets the Sky

It's the canopy
that holds us still;
the blue is dependable,
always there,
it keeps our feet on the ground
and so, a slit in the blue
becomes a slit in the self.

For one whole life,
I ran from the signs,
or they from me;
a whole life,
I was trapped in a yarn
they spun.

Like a dog
spinning in circles,
I chased my tail,
God-like, they watched,

a fly in a trap,
sport for wanton boys,
bait for their play.

It begins in the mind, the fissure
the single seed, the stirring of a doubt,
the question you can't sleep off
or laugh away.

My life has felt
like a suture too ready
to close upon itself
(a surgeon always waiting in the wings?)
Before I could feel the pain
the wound was stitched
the flaps closed
even before
they came undone.

A life's worth of practice
amounts to something, after all;
dodging the little perfections,
beating the trickery
of their seamless machines,
tripping the clockwork
of this make-believe world,
this mockery I called my life
I smiled through the silicon sunshine
of my choreographed days,
I weathered the rage of their calibrated storms,

broke the dam of their monstrous waves
castle walls
of their vain egos.

It feels like the end of some pilgrimage,
saint in sight at last.
Ten steps to the sky,
ten steps to what?
To the truth?
And what would they have done,
a last stab—
folded the great blue canopy,
my sole anchor,
cunningly
upon itself.

# Daughter of the Night:
# Elegy for Shukri Abidi

I see you still
eyes closed.

I hear your silence
louder than my screams
before the wave's final claim.

Where I come from, when elders sang songs to us at night,
they told us we were daughters of the night,
it was always deep, dark moonless night our bodies
deep dark moonless our faces deep dark moonless.

From night's womb I came
brief day
you threw me back in its jaw
deep dark sunless the waters deep dark sunless the waves.

before the passing
so deep.

# Prison

Three words
unsaid—
how many spirits
they keep trapped on earth.

# The Front Yard Blossom

I was so angry at the neighbor's boy
who plucked the pink blossom
off my front yard tree—
one of the only two
on that lone tree
that spread in its majesty
across the breadth of my huge windows.
I almost wept for my lost blossom.


One morning, a wink shorter than forgetting later, I look out,
the whole tree is dotted with pink
enough to carpet the yard,
the tips of the laden boughs kissing the ground
in pink overwhelm.

# Cauldronful of Soul

should I get up to make your tea, you say?
because you won't inconvenience yourself?
lift the velvety tea cozy, pour the tea
from the slender porcelain pot
while holding the lid
from falling at the knob
then fill up every cup with the golden brew
pass it through the strainer's filigree
lift the sugar cubes with thumbelina tongs
plop a dainty brick or two
in every cup, then throw in a splash of milk
smoking hot, watch it trickle, stop
when the colour is juusst right
and someone's hand or someone's word clips my act as if
I didn't know better
stir the cup with a tiny silver spoon, recuperated relic from a
     doll's house or Mad Hatter's party that Alice missed then
     hand out every cup
in the midst of oohs and aahs while everyone applauds
the victory

of the perfect most perfect perfectest cup of tea

could everyone just get up
and serve themselves
for while you fret over your kettles and your teacups
I've got a cauldronful of soul
simmering—do you mind?

# Life's a Soap on My Television Screen

As I watch my city bleed on the television screen
from my three-seater couch,
I feel a new-age, digital-like sorrow—lukewarm,
enough to flatter the conscience
but not to trouble the mind,
enough to tug at the heartstrings
but not to cause any pain.

The balancing is tricky, so
I keep the vista of my vision
cluttered with distractions and playthings;
coke cans and ketchup,
pizza and pearls,
souvenirs from blindfolded travels—
Eiffel Towers in plaster of Paris,
Chinese vases made in Taiwan.

I hop from black to white, obliterate the gray
I appropriate the knowledge according to my mood;
a bit of bloodshed, a bit of jazz,
some song and dance, some war and peace…
one way, it gets too much, too dark
for a sunshine bloke like me.

The world's a stage and
life's a soap on my television screen
the drama folds and unfolds
and all I do is behold
while my conscience is doped;
it's a vaudeville with human puppets,
a little crude at times,
I can handle it pretty well though
I just need my shot;
between murders and musicals,
zapping in and out at will.

# The Knowledge of Rain in My Bones

The twitch, the tug,
I yearn to reach across.
There seems promise in the unseen,
there seems lure in the unscaled.
Distant stars call to me across a blackening sky.
I pick a nascent scent
of something to be born,
like the smell of rain before rain,
like the smell of joy.
The scent of possibility infuses me
like the knowledge of rain saturates a cloud.

They tell me it's okay, they tell me it's all good.
'You got it all', they say,
'You're blessed to have what you have'.

They scare me with Biblical, religious sounding words;
unfaithful, ungrateful, irresponsible, discontent, misfit,
    arrogant.

They do the teacherly act of bulging eyelids and the wagging
     finger,
give me the silent treatment, follow it up
with threats of desertion.

They rain their abstract nouns on me like a third-grade gram-
     mar lesson
to baffle my imagination.
They know I can't find
the consolation of a picture to clip the endless echo
of long empty syllables.

Stranded in a desert? Alone on an island? The butt of jokes?
Society's fool?
Faint pictures come and go
like an ill-orchestrated sequence. I feel no fear, I feel no threat;
all I feel is
the knowledge of rain in my bones

the ripple of something birthing inside me
the force of all those drops.

I want with all my being to take the plunge
and be soaked.

# Window-faced

He comes home one day,
window-faced,
my six-year old,
joyous at his first ever fallen tooth
the neat square of absence sitting on his face
like a single window
in a house from a freak fairy tale
un self-conscious
of its numerical oddness.
It lets in the wind all unevenly
and his tongue slips into the gap
all too often
slurring his speech
spilling the sounds all over,
a gush of hisses and whistles
slipping like miniscule pearls
through the perfect square drain.

# Dusting Symbols

We dust our china
but not our symbols.

What do we bow to
when we bow to Mecca?

# The Man and the River

It was a T-junction on the bed
of the moribund Ravi.
You'd park your beat sedan here in the yawn of night,
drag the bodies from the trunk,
trail them across the gravel, mostly face-down,
lay them at the river's mouth.

This river was a reluctant keeper of secrets;
it wouldn't rush to swallow like a hungry beast with a belly on fire.

Its waters were sluggish and brown,
bogged by centuries of flotsam.
It wouldn't lean in to devour the prey,
instead, its brackish waves would approach
in a whimsical saunter
and poke the feed with feeble waves
like a calculated caress.

I sat long past they had floated away and wondered

Can men change course like rivers?

# In a Suable World

I would sue you
for turning your back
when everyone else had done so too.

I would sue you for every moment that felt like a year,
for every unending second of despair
when it felt like
I was living under a dark rock
with no crevice to let in the light.

I would sue you for the hurt that hurt so much
that I had no choice
but to harden my heart to stone
to keep it from bleeding
like an open wound.

I would sue you
for the years I couldn't bring myself to trust others or myself
because it felt stupid to have done so before.

In a suable world, I would sue you for betraying me
when you knew you were the last man standing
after everyone had stabbed me in the back,
left me bleeding and walked away
all the while knowing I was counting on you.

# Finishing

the body is anchored after a manic march
through choppy seas
a balm sweet as honey soothes the limbs
the soul, aflutter and excited for long
returns home like a nesting bird
the rhythm of being is a gentle steady beat
the unambitious bobbing of an anchored ship
in the calm of a night ocean poised and still
as the night sky
grounded
the motions of flight ended
bare
slipper-spoiled soles
kissing
the dewy velvet of grass

# No-hassle Deal

I only wanted my money's worth and peace of mind,
no questions asked, no pick and drop, just a hassle-free deal
clean
crisp
no 'he loves me, he loves me not'
no pools of lovey dovey eyes
no time wasted on silly, girly stuff
no trouble of flowers and ribbons
hit and run,
done, forgotten, sealed
business-like
twenty-first century style.

I picked her up from Liberty and took her to Ali Shah's place
    (that house like a wedding cake where everyone went).
We drove in steely silence:
it was my first time doing it this way, transaction-like.
Come to think of it, the silence was no less
awkward than the meaningless chatter on a regular date.

She was sultry and aloof,
Scarlett Johansson like.

She gave me her body, but underneath her skin,
her soul steeled like a shield;
one pair of lips she opened,
the other she locked out of reach.
I tried to kiss her; she jerked her face away
with a panther's flair.
She was stone-lipped the entire time. I asked her name,
no answer.

Those mounds rose like summits
that mark a country's border
unscalable
insurmountable
rivulets of a watered down milky white
flowed from them
like feeble fleecy snow trickling down mountain tops.

In the last throes of my ecstasy, as I moaned and convulsed,
	she was still as a slab.
The deed over, I touched her, she was
cold marble of mausoleums.

I got more than I bargained for—
this girl for hire, this woman who was supposed to be
a forgettable number,
by refusing to surrender,
had left me impotent for life.

# Plasma

Sundown is litmus,
the cruelest hour to bear.
'The silence can get too loud'
'The TV will drown the silence.'

The way light fell on it
in that lounge like a cavern,
it was always our own silhouettes we saw
in the backdrop of talk shows and dramas.
Our shrinking frames were drowning in that large, looming
    house.

Sometimes we felt there was a link
between the guilt of those who had left
and the size of the TV screens that arrived.

'Fragile', they said. 'Handle with care.'

# Lines and Circles

I guess you could make a point by sketching a line, slashing
  a surface in two... the trouble with lines is there's always
  two sides, always a feel of *us* and *them*, always a nagging
  polarity, always an either-or kind of chemistry

fences tell you where not to look, they're a stamp of territory,
  you trespass if you overstep,
there's always someone turning away from barbed wires, and
  someone wanting them to stay

when you draw a line between two countries, you force them
  into a posture of self- conscious nationalism, they might
  have a long shared history, they may be cut of the same
  fabric of soul and soil, but you axe them with the blade
  of geography and divide them into parts ... ribs, chops,
  tailbone

lines close deals, terminate possibilities

there's no getting around the notion of otherness, there's no

way to avoid the concept of separateness: what is in me
   that makes me me? what is in you that makes you you?
you are always the other, you are all that is separate and
   strange
you are not what I see when I look in the mirror, you are
   meant to be feared


there is a consolation in the andness of circles, the elasticity
   of their girth, the promise that it can expand without
   snapping like an infinitely stretchable rubber band that
   goes a long way,
lasts a long time, holds many things together in a huddle


a circle will stretch and shrink like water, mould itself in the
   color of the subject, expand or contract its contours, ne-
   gotiate its borderlands, rewrite its geography, their expan-
   sion is the added measure of tiny blessings of tolerant
   nudges and tweaks, the circle isn't threatened if anoth-
   er man walks into its sphere or walks out, it will gladly
   oblige,
it has nothing to lose


with circles, there's always the comfort of possibility, a soften-
   ing of harsh edges
their orbit is a world—
a matriarch's embrace

# Role Play

For how many years
will the same old roles
of conqueror and conquered
play out between us?

How many years
since that first anchored ship?

# Coffee Mornings

They keep sipping coffee,
they keep feeling empty.

# Daliesque

Scrolling through the news, the image strikes you as a painting by Dali, a strangely abstract thing among the strangely concrete – a black blob splayed on the curb, like play-dough melting in the sun. Between her abaya and the road, her flesh had such little mass, such little weight of being, she could be a rag swept up by the wind. She had shunned the advances of a prince who stalked her in a shopping mall. When they were done with her, his men threw her out on the footpath, like tissue they wiped their snot with. The sleek black limo glided on, its dark mirrors rolling up soundlessly.

you are addicted to the thrill of conquest
the rush of adrenaline
the pulse, the heat, the rage
when you knock an opponent down
pin him to the ground
hold up your victor's fist
command the crowd
some ancient instinct from beyond the portals

of consciousness memory
and grasp
unfathomable
nebulous
like the origin of the world
like the presence of god
like the sting of conscience
some primal curve
in the dancing tendrils of your inheritance
the whim of a curve holds the imprint
of an instinct
a tendril dictates
the charge of your blood
tells you you must win
tells you no one dare stand up to you

and she was a mere willow
reed
slip of a girl who dared, said no
a jerk of the head a turning away
a refusal unleashed the beast in you
you broke like the waters of a dam
the chords
the bindings of humanity
the unsigned pact of our simple understandings
you had to have her
you had to taste her body
devour her flesh
chew her guts like chowder
masticate her marrow, crush her jugular
like an animal you had hunted

see her dignity
bleed through her eyes

she was so whole
you had to smash her like a tea cup
so every chip every shard
every icicle of porcelain would calcify your victory
you couldn't crush her spirit
because her soul was granite
ageless timeless marble
so you muddied her flesh
perishable matter
the skin between her legs was wasted muslin now battered
    limp by your assaults
until every spent bit of her was breathless and defeated
a broken mirror multiplies the experience of joy or grief,
it echoes the same truth back to you
in a million shades in a million ways
it hurts back the memory of a single hurt in so many ways it
    feels like
a million wounds hurting

when you had seen
enough proof of your victory
when every shrapnel
of her soul had testified
when every ravished fiber had ceded to you
when your ego was stoked enough for a kill
when the dance of the helix had stilled
you rolled her up
like a bundle

disposable rag
and spat her on the curb
splayed
lonely lonely pancake
fungus-crusted
two-stepped
Daliesque

# Gladiator

Mother,
when I behave myself,
I feel
like a gladiator
trapped in a tiffin.

# Vortex

Back where I'm from,
the afternoon is like a dimension;
you crawl in through one end
and crawl out the other
with half the day gone.

# My Revenge Upon the City

When night falls,
I take my revenge upon the city.

This city that shuts me in in the light of day,
this city, where I cannot sleep on the grass unharrassed,
where I cannot picnic in the park without alarm,
whose squares and public places are closed for my leisure
unless I am leaning on a man's arm.

This city, where on a hot summer's day
I cannot sit on the marble mosaic of a fountain's periphery
next to where the birds come for a sip
and dip my toes in the cool water
without being assailed by a swarm.

This city, where while waiting for a bus
I cannot perch on a bench

and read my Faiz and Turgenev without spiky elbows
shooting down my sides.

This city, where I cannot meditate on the footpath
without a bunch of brats whacking me on my head
as they speed by on their bikes.

When night falls,
I take my revenge upon the city.
I slip into a deep magenta robe
I put on a golden crown and step out into the city
as if I hold dominion over it.

Then, free as a bird, I twirl through the avenues
where now no men lurk
behind wheels,
leering and ogling with their stares and smirks.

I sit by the fountain
and dip my feet into the water.
There are no birds now but I'm happy in the quiet.

I sit on the bus stop outside and read Turgenev out loud.
There is a feeble glow of unsteady might
a quivering circle of light
as my voice bellows out into the night
from my unlikely pulpit.
The few pedestrians headed home after a hard day's work
keep turning back and looking

all the while, walking faster away
as if they've seen a ghost.

At last, my throat dries, I throw my head back, stretch my
    legs and
take a languorous sip (like they do in those commercials
    where time stops for you
to take an unhurried sip).

Then, I eat my warm-toasted sandwich savouring every bite
with an indolence to remind Keats of his odes' might.
Then, cross-legged, on the footpath I sit
squarely facing the road with no traffic.

Just before the crack of dawn, I step home, Turgenev and all.

My revenge on the city is over.

# To the Painter in Amélie Poulain

Broken china
held together
by the miracle of breath.

# Attempt at Apology

Forgive me
that it left you broken too;
there isn't room enough
in the universe
for a mother
to break and unbreak.

# The Roof Over Her Head

She couldn't keep a roof over her head
all life long;
it kept slipping away,
like the ground beneath her feet.

She called them her family but they were pariahs;
they sucked her dry.
She worked like a mule
 to feed and clothe them.

At weddings and funerals,
she borrowed more money than she could repay
working night and day.

First her husband drank her earnings away.
He lay on a charpoy all day long.
Never got a job, never needed to,
because she was a ready slave.

She earned, cooked and cleaned and still bore
the stinging wrath of his 'manly' fury.
Under one excuse or another
he hurled empty wine bottles at her.
She bore it all
like a fate written and sealed.

In between her strife,
she also found the time
to bear his children
to the full count of five.
She never had time to raise them.
They grew up under the lazy eye of a perennially
     drunk father—
always angry, always full of hate.
Then, one day, he passed away.

Everyone told her to secure the house,
for her children were grown up
and could very well play foul.
She didn't listen, she never did.

They got married,
treating her like a rag,
nice to her only when they had a plan
to swindle her again.
Everyone saw right through it,
except her, she never did.

She recently buried a daughter with gangrene in her leg.
She mourned for a few minutes and was back on her double
   shift
the next day. (Who has the luxury to mourn?)

Her life will come full circle soon—
if you call it a life,
this cycle of abuse.
She could never keep a roof over her head all life long;
it kept slipping away,
like the ground beneath her feet.

# When You Went to the Waters

(for Ophelia, Ahsan, and others who went to the waters)

When you gave up on earth
and went to the waters,
what was that grief so large
that no human heart could hear,
could bear?

How long was the journey
from your last familiar step
to your first unknown one?
The element that welcomed you,
was it kinder than the one
that had betrayed you?

Were the waters warm, pale blue,
speckled with sunlight,

or cold and dark
like a motherless world?

Your pain unprisoned, when it fled
the trappings of your last human breaths,
did it glide fish-like into the tide?

Are you lighter now?

# Murder of an Autumnal Paris Evening

There was a girl in Khaadi
under the Eiffel Tower;
her dress kept stabbing
the evening's grey heart
like a rainbow-coloured sword.

# Heaven Bound

A sliver of a moment
between this world and the next,
snug around my abdomen,
the portal between the twain.

# You Give Up on Your Homeland When

Being loyal to it
feels like
betraying
yourself.

# We Could Never

We could never meet
in the mind;
some quirk of the flesh
always kept us.

# Some Men

Some men,
when they see me on the road,
grind their teeth so hard,
make their engines growl so loud,
I know
they've ground me to
gravel in their minds.

# A Horde, a Nation

From afar,
you can mistake
one for the other.

# In the Time Before the Walls

There was only
realm
beyond
realm.

# Continents Breaking

She had left the house with a week's change of clothes and a dozen frozen meat patties. (You don't pack smart when you're a land mass coming loose.)

Then she sent me to collect the rest of her stuff. It was so hard climbing those once-familiar stairs.
I tried to sweep up all her things and stuff them in the car trunk. An armful is an armful, poor measure to apportion a lifetime of spoils.

She held the ministry of memories. She was always the caretaker of moments. The family pictures were stacked neatly in albums, ordered by years. They were covered in a sheet of plastic as if to ensure that the moments were kept air-tight, sealed, so no instance of togetherness could escape.

The stacks stuck together; the moments came undone.

As I balanced one load in my arms, an album fell on the
ground, and a sealed symphony broke free. It was that
music trapped in boxes, when you open them, a ballerina
moves ever so slowly in a full circle. It is the music of
the stream of memories, the tune of sealed bliss. It is the
music of happily ever after.

I heard it years later, in a song I was listening to in a new
language, a language I was growing into. Did the music
mean the same thing in every language? Did it always
promise that things will come full circle, then watch your
heart break when time didn't keep its word?

*Le temps est assassin / Et emporte avec lui le rire des enfants / Et
les mistrals gagnants.* (Time is a grim reaper / and steals the
laughter of children / and free childhood treats.)

The false music of eternity couldn't hold together the self that
was coming undone. It gave a cadence to the free fall,
brought a rhythm to the breach as you shatter on the
inside;
I shattered, but I shattered rhythmically.

They were still together on that page – young, and full of
hope.

I want a lesson in courage from cartographers and the clean-
ers of battlefields, those who tackle the flux of frontiers,
those who sweep the spoil of battle, as the sides keep
changing.

I am unable to cut along dotted lines memories that are burnt
into my veins. I am unable to unthread the skein of mo-
ments that is my skin.
I fail to nip and tuck the geography of the self.

How long before no mist of memories mars the windswept
battle sites? How long before the earth is healed of the
tremors of continents breaking?

# Sundays

I knew it was a new chapter
when the meaning of my Sundays changed.

# Which Black Hole

Into which black hole go
the email addresses of the dead
the burdens of the heart
that is finally at rest
the dregs of dreams
that failed life's test
promises made but not kept

the chorus of goodbyes unsaid?

# Earth

His body
when
he makes love
to me.

# Teenage

The ease of his goodbyes
breaks my heart.

# What Grandma Knew

Grandma used to say
man is a snake
up your sleeve.
I thought she was a bitter old hag
until it was too late—
I was foaming at the mouth.

# Object of Envy

I envy men
the codes
of their friendships.

# Foresight

The way some mothers
treat their daughters, it seems
they're training them
for the pain to come.

# Idols

So many idols rose and broke
one left me broken too.

# Razzmatazz

Mecca

Manhattan

# Simile

As stubborn as a poet's heart

# Question Across Time

To the first little girl
who betrayed another
for a boy's attention,
do you know how much
your legacy costs the world?

# Superglue

Time

# Maulvion Waali Kothi (The House With the Bearded Men)

Bathed in a crisscross
of moon beams through the lattice,
the rooftop looked like a backdrop
for an alien ship landing.

Her nervous fingers stopped twitching
at the shuffle of footsteps.

He bent down and kissed away
an errant tress from her creamy breast.

Till long into the waning moonlight,
the only sounds in the air
were the fireflies singing and love juices meeting.

For twenty years,
they had kept up this rite

of meeting here every Friday night
while down below in the house,
everyone slept,
children and all.

# Cleanse

The silence when
all the screams
have been screamed.

# White Man

He struts into the room
like he owns it,
sprinkles his opinion
everywhere
like urine.

# Pauper

Those who held open the doors
of his diamond-studded Royce
spat on his shadow
when he had gone.

# Waltz

Standing in the line
at the grocery store,
underneath her abaya,
she was dancing
discreetly to Chantaje.

# Neighborhood

Sharks:
first they sniff for blood,
then they come in for the kill.

# Kinds of Giving

When a small man gives,
it's a noose around the neck.
When a big man gives,
it's a rain from the heavens.

# Feminazi

She was so tired
of wanting to be fully loved,
so tired of turning
every betrayal
into a conference paper;
all that was soft in her
had hardened now;
her defenses had blocked
all pathways
where love could have flown.

# The Writer's Fate

Your words will be forgotten

# Dead Poet

An unfinished octave
lay paused in his pupils.

# Lullaby

Pacing the room with a bay window
in the Manhattan loft,
she was rocking a child in her arms,
singing a lullaby in her native tongue.

Across the skyscrapers,
as her feet paced the cold concrete,
her eyes had wandered to a warmer continent
where palm trees lined the horizon
and flashes of colour
from fishermen's robes
stabbed the eye.

Before her eyes was floating
the image of another
whom she yearned to cradle in her arms,
whom she wanted,
ever so softly, to sing to sleep.

# Metamorphosis

I'm turning into a writer,
this person I always wanted to be.

I sit beyond concrete barriers
fishing poems out of my head,
capturing them in my red Moleskine.

Mid-conversation, I trail off
into the scene of a novel in progress.

That one missing rhyme
from a ballad strikes me
in the most random moment.

Be it wedding or funeral
I'm never without my notebook.

When I go to do my groceries,
I always get the daffodils,
and I always forget the milk.

# Valentine's Day

Their love that lasted half a century,
it wasn't built on flower stalks
wrapped in fancy cellophane.
It rested on the thorns
they had trodden together
that had smeared their feet.

# Butterfly

Gentle,
let it land while still aquiver
with the tremor of life,
its restless flutter tickling your palm,
the colours of its wings steadying
as its little heart trembles.

Those wings are pixie dust;
held too tight,
they are ash,
they are yesterday.

# F.I.R

Robbers
they stole my beautiful belief,
they stole my reason
for jumping out of bed
every morning.

# The Lesson Before the Last

Sore thumb, it was always jammed
like a crowbar between us and our freedom,
the geography lesson,
the lesson before the last.

Miss Relph, she was more arid
than the plains she told us of,
her own relief lacked the tributaries of love,
the rivulets and soft showers
of daily bliss and joy.
Her face had marks
of healed gashes like battle scars
her slit-like lips
no muscle memory of a smile.

She came straight from her Volkswagen into class,
unfashionably earlier than the students,
missing the limelight of the great entrance.

She never lingered in the staff room
for a chai and a chat like the others, never basked,
like the others, in the easy fandom of students.
Like her life, she was parched,
all brown and colourless.

So, on that fateful day in April
when the scent of first blossoms wafted
through the classroom windows,
making the wait even harder,
what is this we see?

Miss Relph, drier than the desert of Namibia,
enters, smiling faintly, cautious creases
forming at the corners of her lips
in the unpractised gesture of a smile.

On the board, bang top center,
where she always writes the chapter head
in her steady Convent cursive
and draws a straight line underneath with gusto,
'I mean business, goddamit', it says.
Today, instead of 'Dormant Volcanoes',
she slowly writes 'I do',
the chalk lingering too long
at the north-eastern flick of her 'o'.

# Half and Half

Worlds floated in her eyes;
when she blinked,
a hemisphere was eclipsed.

# Becoming Bird

tremor in the feather
steadies
wing
becomes blade
slices the air
blade of knife
gliding
through sap of aloe

# What the Fire Couldn't Take From Us

Promises of youth
are matters of life and death,
so serious the world would end at the slightest unrest.

The night before the ballet in the amphitheater,
our rehearsal turned out to be a final act.

At least we all left together
joined forever by the clumsiness of rosy promises
untested against the litmus of time;
to see what sheds, what remains,
to know words too easily spoken
from promises made and kept.

Fire is a great leveler,
treating man and brick alike.

The robes our mothers had sewn for us
lay hanging in our closets.

The painter painting his series on dancing youth
needed only two colours for his canvas today
– orange blaze with billows of black rumbling.

Youth is angry, youth is restless,
it states the obvious,
it craves closure.

And so we returned a last time,
our acts now second nature,
our motions fluid,
memories not failing
the slightest remembrance.

We had it, our last dance –
the one thing the fire couldn't take from us.

# How To Defrost a Chicken

I would always be stumped
by the unyielding mass, club-like,
the pieces stuck together
defying discernment,
all fourteen of them.

I'd submerge it in a bowl and pray,
hoping for the circuits to battle it out
while I looked the other way.

Often, half a day would go by
before I dared to check in
on the progress.

A wise woman
taught me how to do it
in under ten minutes.

'It is only at the joints
that the ice is unrelenting,
pry it open with your fingers
and the rest will come undone.'

'Always
a fault-line
where the crust
is hardest,' she said. 'Always look
for where
there is sediment un-addressed.'

# The Keen-eyed One

They float in her eyes now,
the clouds, lakes of milk
that you and I will likely get at her age.

Her memory is hazy and sharpened in parts,
giving her life a strange reset.
She'd skip a generation when remembering kin,
take her grandson for her son.
She'd need a map for her own home,
lose her way from room to kitchen.
But remember the count of roses
in the lone bush that bloomed last week,
the extra pinch of salt in yesterday's lunch,
whom to blame for it.

It's not like before, talking to her;
you never know
what to expect any more.
All you can do is
cast fragments in a muddy lake

and hope for something to hold.
She plumbs the depths,
scanning for a match of memory.
Some random bits will click,
across her eyes a flash will flit
before they cloud over again,
waking already to stranger worlds perhaps.

Back in the day,
when these same servants
who look through her today
used to tremble at her command, she would pull out
pictures of her younger self –
proud, fiery-eyed, sharp-jawed, back held straight.

There was a cliché in her tongue
she was fond of using.
'My eye was so keen', she would say
'I could count the feathers of a bird in flight.
Where one ended, the other began, from this far below,
I could trace the seam.'

# Two Sides

At the Indian joint,
the old man who walked in
had a telltale sleepiness
in his eyes;
he looked at everything
through a screen of longing,
a half-formed smile
of retreat—
young couples fretting
over spoonfuls of food,
babies sleeping,
the bustle in the place,
the business of life.

There were two sides already;
he stood on one,
life, on the other.

# Karachi

They say you can take the man out of the city,
but not the city out of the man.

It echoes behind my ear drums
muffled boom of bullet
dulled by window glass
rattle of gun
raining in the dead of night.

It lies behind my eyes
garden of corpses strewn,
red of bloom,
red of doom confused.

It breaks my sleep
spell of sweat
as I wake, hapless,
from a dream of fear.

It trails inside my mind
like a silent snake

the ever-present fear that
no matter where I am
someone is following close behind.

It beats in my temples
a remembered rub
the graze of muzzle
cheek of metal kissing cheek of man.

The city is lodged,
second mind within my mind.

They were right.
You can take the man out of the city
but not the city out of the man.

# The President
# and the Pin

'When your mother lives for the country,
get used to not having her around.'
'A country's fate is greater than a man's.'
'My time with you is a gift,
my allegiance is to my country.'

When the soldiers' boots thundered
at the door that night,
she was still,
her soup untouched before her.
In their last few steps till the threshold,
she had stiffened her neck (as if sensing the blade),
and murmured a prayer.

From her breast,
she had unpinned her martyr's brooch
and whispered in a stable voice,
'Clasp this every time you waver,

every time you feel you're coming undone.
A country's fate is greater than a man's.'

Whenever I speak to my country, the brooch is in my hand.

# Frame

There was already the story
of the people in sepia—
two women and a man
leaning against the bonnet of a Bentley,
an England street behind them.
To that, the ghosts of droplets
that had dried across the surface,
edges of the picture swollen and curled,
added another frame.

# French 101: Syntax of Missing

*Manquer* (verb): to miss
Example:
*Tu me manques*: You (from me) are missing = I miss you

Not the idle kind of missing,
where you sit like a pining lover,
and miss something from a distance.

This is another kind of missing.
The thing is missing from you.
It became a part of you,
so that when you miss it,
you become un whole, incomplete
un yourself.

Think of it like this—every missing burns
an object-shaped hole in the body.
When a dish is missing salt,

there's a salt-shaker-shaped hole in the plate.
When you miss a father who's no more,
all of you is a gaping hole,
smarting with an absence
larger than anything you've ever known.

# Pirate Filter

Always a good idea
to spunk up the holiday pics
with a filter.
Nothing screamed fun, beach, sand, and sun,
like the wantonness
of buntings or a rainbow.

She tried several,
all fell short one way
or the other—
Mickey, Rapunzel, Frozen, and glitter.

The pirate filter worked best,
she found; the patch hid the spot
where he had given her a blue eye.

# A Prayer for the Butcher

With regular ones, he takes liberties,
draws out the chats, with finicky ones,
he'll go a step further,
throw in a tease or two to sweeten the deal.

'Only for you, the choicest cut.
Two packs per chicken, just as you like.
I won't go the trouble for everyone, you are special.
Say a prayer for me in turn.'

'Just did, and always will.'
I said in what I thought
was a fiercely reciprocal bid.

'Tell me. What did you pray for?'
He wanted to vet
the contents of my prayer, as if there was
anything else I could ask for, besides

a happy home, grateful children,
enough to live by, peace in his heart,
the least and the most we all could ask for.

Of all our utterances on earth,
a prayer is, perhaps,
the easiest
to work into a template.

# The Belly Dancer

White waves undulating
from breast to belly,
waist guarded like a treasure
in a cast of chimes, practiced beats
on her small feet,
red-painted toes ringed.

Aware, like a goddess,
of the spell she cast
in the room.

How many times
had they undressed her in their minds,
run their fingers
on her dimpled flesh,
pried open the cast that chained her navel.
Their eyes had glazed over, they were gods,
towering over her.

In the gaze of the women,
there was a journey
from fear to envy then defeat.

After some time,
between what she read in the eyes
of men and women,
there was no difference at all.

# Cakes by Carol

It brought a strange comfort;
somewhere in the folds of fondant
she felt she had stowed away
dreams she had held on to for too long,
dreams she was too tired to carry any further.

She was happiest when the show was on,
in worlds lit up briefly by candles,
ending when the pantomime
was put out by breath.
What did it matter then?
No matter the spectacle,
it was spoof in the end,
a farce made real,
made larger than life
by the dance of smoke.

smokescreen
sugar-screen

She had dreamt of building
towers of concrete
like the models
in her childhood room and here she was,
learning to balance layers of cake
on stilts of sugar.

A twenty-first century woman,
she had thought, breadwinner,
independent, all words
reserved for men.
Instead of big, fat cheques
that made the world go around,
she was dealing in sprinkles and chocolate chips.
Instead of heading the boardroom,
she was ushered as an excuse, a side act,
like the clown, only sadder.

They were the real deal, mommies in Lululemon
who placed the orders sliding seamlessly
from treadmills to skyscrapers,
suited-up or stripped down at command,
daddies who came gliding in limousines
and told her to keep the change,
always in a hurry to leave the block.

Her job? Making replicas from replicas,
a painter copying the artefacts of maestros.
She was playing in miniature
what she had failed to play in real.

Google the picture of a perfect life and build it in marzipan.
Air bubbles have texture when treated right.
Stiff peaks of egg whites,
could they hold a monument on their weight?
A monument to abandoned dreams,
a Madonna sculpted in dregs.

She needed the sweetness to swallow the evening
before the evening swallowed her whole.
They were balm for her soul,
the corners she shaved off the sponge,
odd angles ousted
by the recipe's decree.

Those hours passed like thorns
when the kids were asleep
and the man still mid-way
between work and home; every day
she deferred a meeting with herself.
The times she caught her image in the hallway mirror,
it was a ghost she saw,
wrapped in a shroud of castor sugar,
the dirty kitchen of 'Cakes with Carol'.

He had begun to avert his eyes at the diabetes ad;
she was way more skilful in avoiding the truth.

No amount of sugar could sweeten
what had curdled deep inside her.

# What Dreams May Come

She could not
do what they did,
those girls on the screen,
slick-bodied,
nimble tricks up their sleeves.

It was planted between them
forever, this knowing,
when they were together, when apart.

Every day, as she went through the motions,
every night, as they lay back to back,
screams of strange women
haunting the dreams of both.

# Omen

We kept behaving as if
we were packing for another trip;
he kept shaking his head
as if
we were leaving for another life.

# Archive

Only when I go through
the black and white pictures
in the old shoebox
do I realize
there was a time
when she was someone
other than my mother.

# Bargain for Loss

The signs were always there
for willing ones to see
never a cliché
without a grain of truth.

At the end of the day, all you'll be
is the governess, the nanny—
meant to depart
at a preset hour.

The night-time snuggles
are only for the mother,
for her, the heart-breaking tenderness
of her child breathing at her nape.

You will sleep alone
in a cold bed
your body hungry
for a love whose time is past.

How they tried to make me see
the finality of the regret
when youth is past, spent,
the hope of a hearth your own
a man by your side
the sounds of children
to keep you alive
before the evening gulps you down.

All you'll have
is a worn satchel
tokens, like dried-up flowers
of a love that felt eternal
at the time—you,
a role model
lone heroine in an apocalypse
of obscenely optimistic palette
the naïveté of a conjured world
long forgotten by the very hands that dreamt it up
minds
that outgrew it.

# New Year's Resolution

It has almost been a year,
time to change their habits.
Teach the eye to stop hovering
at knee-level around the house,
walk the carpet with a mind at ease,
stop fearing the stab
of a loose Lego block,
stop lingering at the bend,
stop staring at the grave at the edge,
the smallest rectangle of them all.

# Messages

I wonder if you are lighter
where you slipped;
summer's round the bend,
I'm sure there will be more sun.

From here, it looks like they go all the way down—
beams of sunlight
diving headlong through the waves.

There was method to it, they kept saying,
seeing your things lined up by the shore.
A verdict the whole city heard,
the whole city that was searching for you.

The bills in the wallet
went from smallest to highest.
We thought you were never listening, that careless air…
for once, you had undone your laces.

The basketball hoop has started to droop.
The boys next door
don't come to play any more.

Sometimes, after rain,
beads gather on the window pane.
I don't let them dry unnoticed
like before.
I don't treat them
like another thing of the world.

I wipe them on my palm.
I like the way it feels on my cheek—water,
the memory of you.

# Idle Blades

Bad omen
*badshagoon*—
scissors
when they snap
idly
cutting air
instead of objects.

Elders used to say
it caused fights in households.

Knives
tongues
scissors—
they're all the same.

Their work is the work of evil
when left unrestrained
So you can blame
a broken home

on scissors,
on blades that snapped on idly
not knowing
whom they hurt
or how much.

# First Bike

At six,
his talking still too much
like birdsong,
he was telling his grand-parents
about his first bike,
accessories
he was saving for—bell-horn, basket,
the full works.

In response to his chirping,
they kept answering
with news
of their own son's bike, my son's father,
a full forty of age.
As if it was fresh from last week,
they told with relived regret
how the bike was stolen
the same week it was bought.

I thought it was a sign
they were going senile,
this time warp they were in.

Yesterday, he left for college again.
Making his bed,
I close the door on
his once-again empty room.

Wasn't it yesterday
taking the third wheel off his bike?
yesterday
his bruise from the first fall?

Life's like that—
you look over your shoulder, it's gone.

# We Were Two Women
in a Room

Across the restaurant,
we were two women in a room,
our lives suddenly face to face.

She was feeding a second child at her breast,
singing a lukewarm *wheelsonabusgoroundandround*
scanning the menu furtively in-between,
Shiva with hands in a hundred places, in her mind,
the hissing rattlesnake of a to-do list,
making her eyes senseless busy,
mist-covered windows.

Baggy pants, baggy shirt;
I remember the time
I had harbored my body in the flowing folds,
I remember when that felt like the only safe place.

I know by the heartache of absence now

that absolute dependence of a body
that came from you, was bound to you –
against your breast,
lining the inside of your mind,
wedged like a tiny nuisance
between you and another
who made love each night
(or was that another life?)

I remember the vertigo,
the merciless falling through space
finding footing
between losing what you thought was a thing of beauty
and watching it become
something from a biology text book,
a vessel through which life fulfilled its purpose.

I remember the strangeness of milk flowing,
I remember the soreness of breasts to the touch.
I remember the inkwell of shame,
the silence you could howl yourself hoarse into,
doors closing with nowhere to run.

How clichéd would it be
to smile to her and say it will go by too fast.
How much he needs you now
hurts nothing like how little he will need you later.
You won't believe me if I told you
the ease of their goodbyes will break your heart.
Time will free up suddenly
like a lake drying up in the sun

you'll find yourself a stupid Jack-in-the-box,
grinning,
head out of water at last,
painted and dressed with nowhere to go
late for the show,
always late for the show.

That's probably how she saw it, look at this woman,
sitting in the middle of a café by herself like a queen,
owning her solitude and her space,
no children to put to sleep,
no duties pulling her a million ways,
what sweet freedom it would be
for a woman to be this free.

We were two women in a room
each looking at the other
thinking how much time had gone.

# Resident Ghost

Over time
the gold leaf will wither
but the imprint of letters burnt in the spine
will stay—
one half of a writer's life,
the realm of forever.

It's with humans as it is with books;
a single column holds the frame in place.

Have you ever tried to erase a father?
Look through him like a ghost,
pretend he wasn't there?
It's impossible to do, he grows back.
Cut him off, and you'll see it's your own limb you lost.

You are never alone
when you walk
somewhere in the back,
the ghost of a father lingers,

too proud for apology
too late for redress.

He'll linger where you least suspect,
haunt you unawares between yourself and yourself,
a voice steadying your cursive as you write,
a remembered tremor from a reprimanding tap
('Stay a certain distance above the line').

Back in the day, it was lost on you
the beauty of a calligrapher's pen
and the standard of the chiseled nib ('Ball points are suicide')
you were too young to value the attention to little things
not knowing what a thing of beauty it was
to have someone look that far out for you.

He is a resident ghost. Listen,
it's his voice in your throat
as you speak to your own son
your voice steadying itself
at a timbre
firm enough to keep him from falling
gentle enough to let him fly.

# I Braided Moonlight
Through Her Hair

On days I was lucky and she would let me,
I braided moonlight through her hair,
the sum of it a tassel that
barely grazed my palm,
her scalp playing peek-a-boo
through the thinning mesh-like strands.
She smelt of roses and remembrances,
things that time hadn't soured.
Since then, I thought heaven's mists
would smell like Tibet Rose.

She was always
only halfway present on earth,
journey-ready for other realms,
part-angel since my earliest memory of her,
well past spite and human grudges,
swimming in forgiveness.

I thought she was weightless,
light enough to be airborne,
yet she fell and broke her hip one day,
then lay on the bed with
a broken-china hip.

Broken bones
turn toxic after some time.
Funny world, you can live with a broken heart all your life,
and die of broken bones in months.

Moonbeams through windowpanes
are streaks of silver I wove through her hair once,
feeling like I was part of a special circle;
she's smiling down from heaven,
looking down from the other end.

# Trigger Warning

That's why we have borders,
from planets to continents to countries.
It's a good idea to keep zones distinct.
They're best when held apart;
there's trouble when they mix,
serious inconveniences
when they bleed into each other.

Let us be sane,
let us maintain these distinctions;
like well-behaved adults,
let us keep our issues separate.

It's all a little muddled
in your hemispheres down under;
things run into each other,
people and nature are often out of control,
laws of universe and governance
can't hold, it seems.

Don't barge in
with your complications, your struggles and abuse.
What's with the South anyway,
what's with you all from down under, always climbing,
always trying to move upwards?

Don't trouble the meticulous tranquility of our hemisphere.
We've built our sanitized worlds with care and calculation;
don't muddy them with the sludge of your woes
with no end or cure in sight.

I can't handle these dark clouds
hovering over my spotless blues.
I need time to remember
there is life beyond my cocoon.
I need time to adjust my reality
I need time to switch my spectacles,
find a new viewfinder,
the empathy exercise what-not,
put myself in your shoes et cetera.

I can't risk
that the trauma trouble me
with issues from irrelevant worlds.
I need a bell,
I need a siren,
I need a trigger warning.

# Punjaban in Calvin Klein

Was that a pout
as you hang the jeans back?
That bowed head,
were you thinking
'I'll never fit into these?'

Why do you care if your contours
defy the rigid geometry
of borrowed wear?
Why do you need to flatten your curves
to fit into miniature grids?

Those thighs weren't made
for the clickety click of pencil heels
through narrow cobblestone streets,
the harried rhythm of cities on steroids;
they were meant for lush green fields
verdant acres without end

they were meant for free-spirited runs
through fields of mango trees.

Your soles kiss the soil
with a settler's timeless pride, full force and gentle
in the primal touch of dust and dust
every clap a salutation
every step an act of salam.
You roam the earth as if
all of it was sacred turf
your ancestral playground.

Your fullness is an arc
drawn back to your ancestors,
a life lived by the simple and visible
labour sowed and bounty reaped,
the cycle of four seasons.

Don't starve your spirit
to fit a preset frame.
You were meant for other scales;
not for you sipping tea with puckered lips,
holding teacups
at slippery fulcrums
of narrow-arched handles,
right hand's pinky stretched.
Your manna came straight from the udder.
You drank bounty
as white as October clouds,
with froth as pearly as
a waterfall's drop.

You drank by the generous gulp,
not the calculated sip,
your wide-rimmed copper glass
cool as the shade of trees on your head
cool as the soil beneath your feet.

Not for you the prudish talk
webs of malice and urban deceit; pure-hearted one,
you only know how to say things as they are;
the truth in your heart
spilling straight from your mouth
before your mind can know.

# Soundtrack
of a Broken Home

It starts as a tear,
then the chasm widens.

Silence is the infill for everything—
what hurts,
what you can't make sense of,
what you hate,
what won't go away.

It's a silence
that turns everything to stone,
a silence that says
it's too late for amends,
laden with the weight of wasted moments;
the debris of unspoken nothings that were
meant to sweeten the everyday
suddenly standing like a dam of concrete,
the swell of the unsaid

pounding at the gates.
Tiny slips added up, each little nothing
grown into its full charge of rage.

Time keeps score,
and the body keeps score.

A perfume from a pilgrimage
becomes a sculpture
through neglect,
lying in the same spot unnoticed,
immortalizing the clumsiness of the giver,
and the refusal of the taker,
frozen in abstraction at that tilted angle
on the drawing room table
where everyone would see it
several times a day
but say nothing and ask nothing.

Ellipses were the coverall
for question marks and full stops,
missing lines of text,
whole pages left blank.

Just when you think
you had mastered the language of silence,
that's when the screams begin
They last all life long.

# Author Bio

Naima Rashid is an author, poet and translator. Her work has been long-listed for the National Poetry Competition and Best Small Fictions. Her published works include critically acclaimed translations of works by Ali Akbar Natiq (*Naulakhi Kothi*) and Perveen Shakir (*Defiance of the Rose*) and a joint translation from French (*Chicanes*). Her work and views have been widely published internationally including in *Wild Court, Poetry Birmingham, The Scores* and *Asymptote*. She lives in the UK with her family. This is her fourth book. At present, she is working on her short story collection and her first novel. Her website is www.naimarashid.com.